DL 2003 OB

DOTS AND LINES, INK.

THE OBOE BOOK

featuring the music of
Chip Davis

9130 MORMON BRIDGE ROAD OMAHA, NEBRASKA 68152 402.457.4341

Published by

DOTS AND LINES INK.
9130 Mormon Bridge Road
Omaha, NE 68152
402.457.4341

Christmas Lullaby

Oboe part edited by Bobby Jenkins

Chip Davis
Arranged for Piano and Oboe by Jackson Berkey

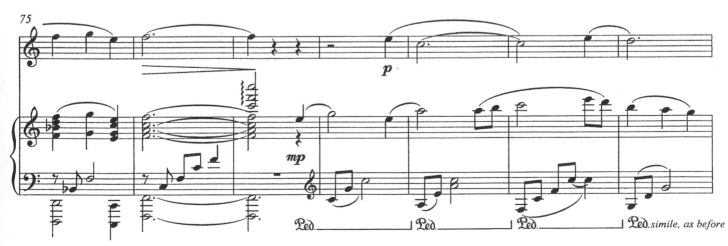

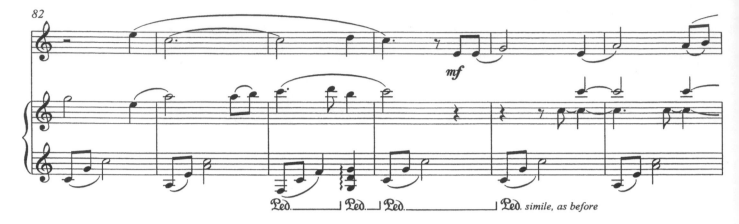

Sun in the Rain

Oboe part edited by Bobby Jenkins

Chip Davis
Arranged for Piano and Oboe by Jackson Berkey

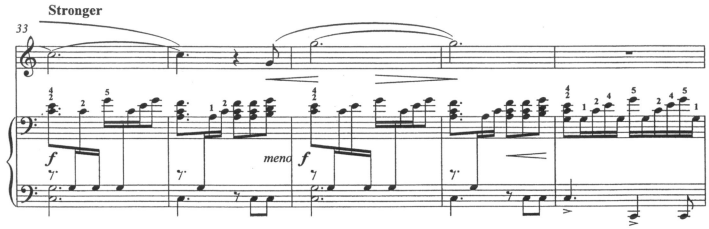

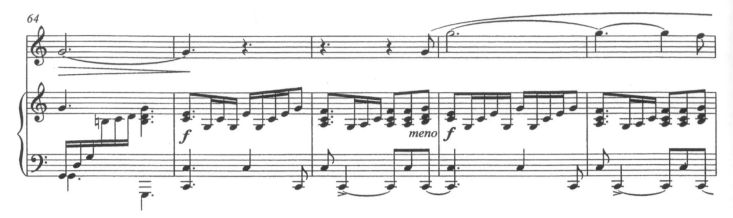

non ritard.

Bittersweet

Oboe part edited by Bobby Jenkins

Chip Davis
Arranged for Piano and Oboe by Jackson Berkey

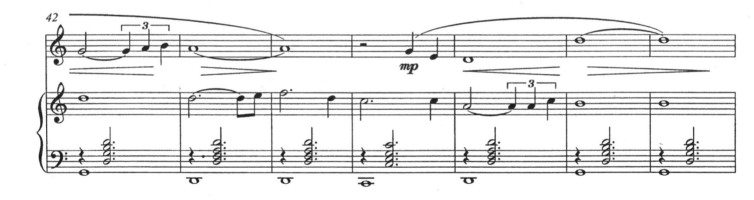

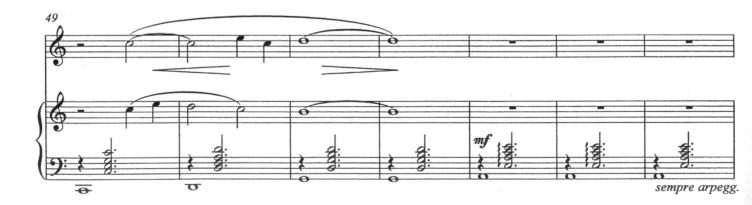

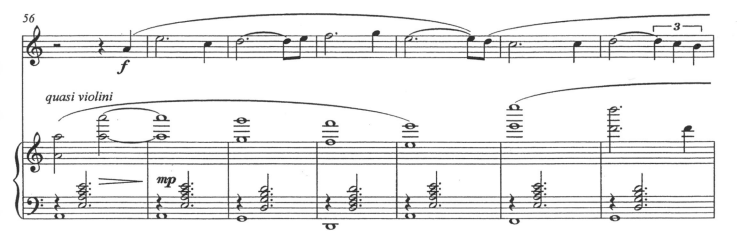

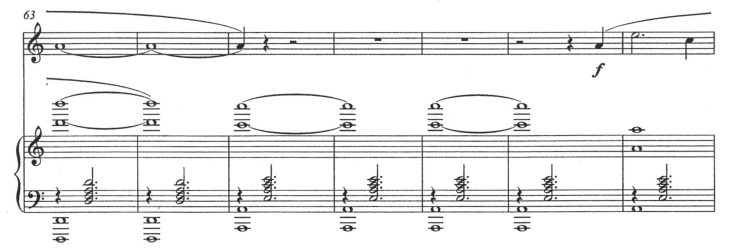

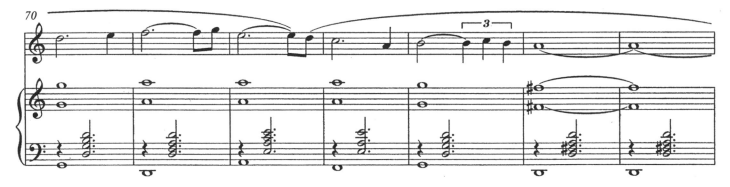

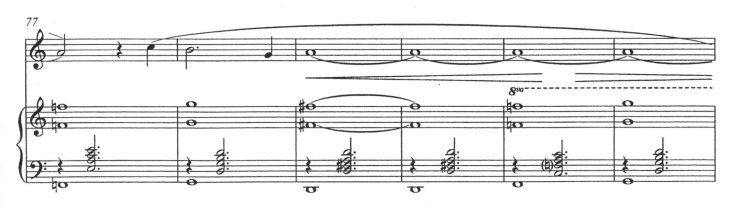

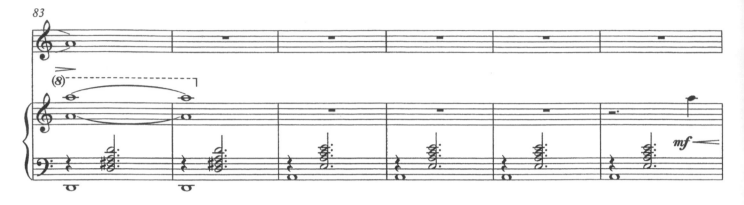

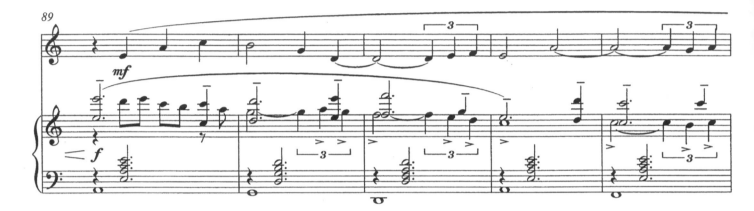

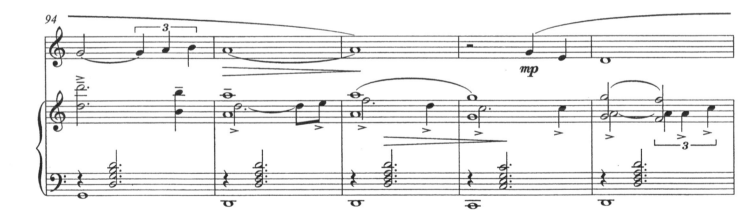

Nepenthe

Oboe part edited by Bobby Jenkins

Chip Davis
Arranged for Piano and Oboe by Jackson Berkey

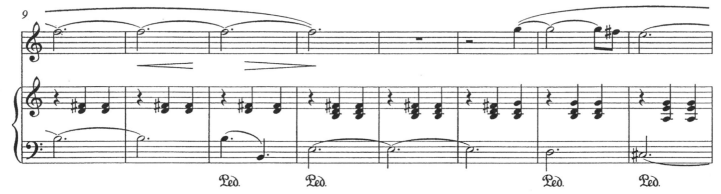

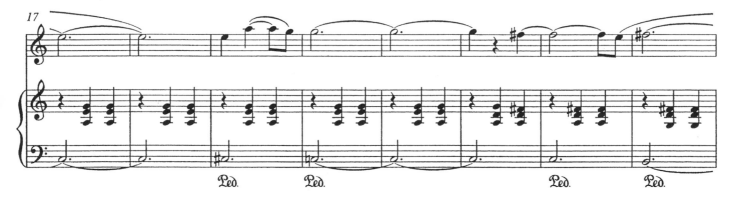

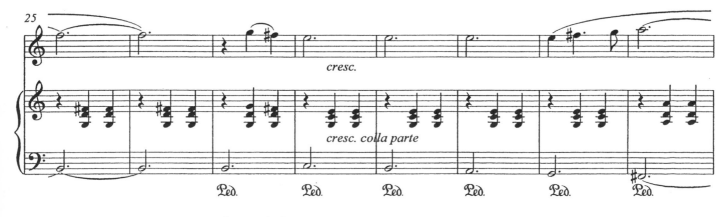

Copyright © 1985 DOTS AND LINES INK.

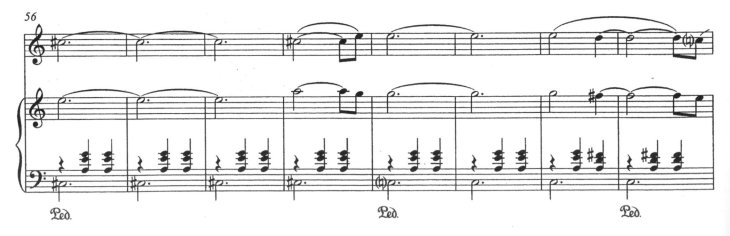

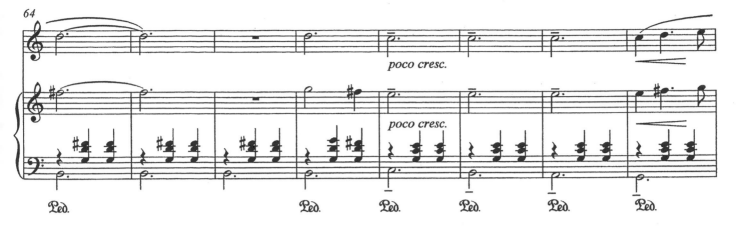

rall.   A tempo

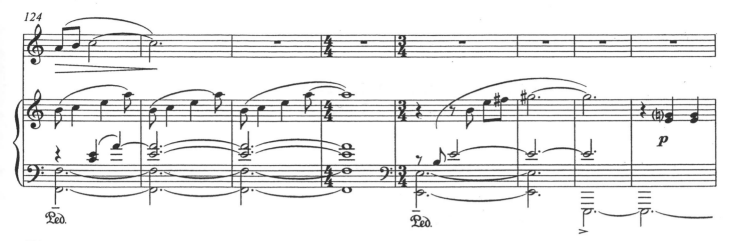

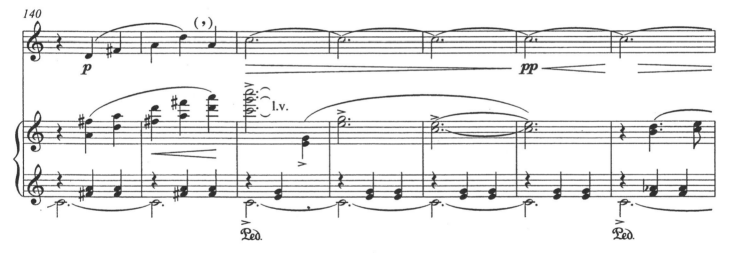

Repeat several times with fade

ALSO AVAILABLE FROM DOTS AND LINES INK. AND HAL LEONARD CORP.

MANNHEIM STEAMROLLER CHRISTMAS (PS 1984 S) $15.95
Arranged by Chip Davis. Solo Piano Transcriptions by Jackson Berkey.

Includes: "Deck The Halls," "We Three Kings," "Bring A Torch, Jeannette, Isabella," "Coventry Carol," "Good King Wenceslas," "Wassail, Wassail," "Carol of the Birds," "I Saw Three Ships," "God Rest Ye Merry, Gentlemen," "Stille Nacht" and "God Rest Ye Merry, Gentlemen" (Rock 'n' Roll).

A FRESH AIRE CHRISTMAS (PS 1988 S) $15.95
Arranged by Chip Davis. Solo Piano Transcriptions by Jackson Berkey.

Includes: "Hark! The Herald Angels Sing," "Veni, Veni," "The Holly and The Ivy," "Little Drummer Boy," "Still, Still, Still," "Lo How A Rose E'er Blooming," "In Dulci Jubilo," "Greensleeves," "Carol of the Bells," "Traditions of Christmas" and "Cantique de Noel" (O Holy Night).

CHRISTMAS IN THE AIRE (PS 1995 S) $15.95
Arranged by Chip Davis. Solo Piano Transcriptions by Hal Leonard Corp.

Includes: "Joy To The World," "Joseph Dear Oh Joseph Mine," "Rudolph The Red Nosed Reindeer," "Herbei, Oh Ihr Gläubigen" (O Come All Ye Faithful), "Pat A Pan," "O' Little Town of Bethlehem," "Angels We Have Heard On High," "Gagliarda," "Los Peces en el Rio," "Christmas Lullaby," "Kling, Glöckchen" and "Jingle Bells."

CHRISTMAS IN THE AIRE (EASY PIANO SOLO) (PS 1995 EPS) $12.95
Arranged by Chip Davis. Solo Piano Transcriptions by Hal Leonard Corp.

Includes: "Joy To The World," "Joseph Dear Oh Joseph Mine," "Pat A Pan," "Herbei, Oh Ihr Gläubigen" (O Come All Ye Faithful), "O' Little Town of Bethlehem," "Angels We Have Heard On High," "Gagliarda," "Los Peces en el Rio," "Christmas Lullaby," "Kling, Glöckchen" and "Jingle Bells."

CHRISTMAS EXTRAORDINAIRE (PS 1225 S) $15.95
Arranged by Chip Davis. Solo Piano Transcriptions by Hal Leonard Corp.

Includes: "Hallelujah," "White Christmas," "Away in a Manger," "Faeries" (Dance of the Sugar Plum Fairies), "Do You Hear What I Hear?," "The First Noel," "Silver Bells," "Fum Fum Fum," "Some Children See Him," "Winter Wonderland," "O Tannenbaum" and "Auld Lang Syne."

DOTS AND LINES, INK.

9130 MORMON BRIDGE ROAD OMAHA, NEBRASKA 68152 402.457.4341

ISBN 0-634-07838-0

0 73999 28972 5

HL00331184

EXCLUSIVELY DISTRIBUTED BY

HAL•LEONARD®
CORPORATION

7777 W. BLUEMOUND RD. P.O. BOX 13819 MILWAUKEE, WI 53213